The historic Red Barn has been saved and works very well as a precious location for displays of early flight history. Who can guess how important this old structure will become to us in the future? The collection within it has expanded beyond the fondest dreams of early enthusiasts, providing for our study some of the most valuable icons of our century. The displays, tracing mankind's indomitable pursuit of flight, are comprehensive. Included with the hardware one will find the stories of human enterprise, successes and failures, the evolution of technology, the building of an industry, and, always, the impact of all of this on us and our world.

We opened The Great Gallery in July 1987 with a big "Welcome!" We want our visitors to have a good time while looking, listening, studying, reflecting, and while participating in the tours, special events and programs. We want you to share our dream. And to dream your own dream of what the future can hold.

Howard Lovering
Executive Director

Rocketry workshops draw enthusiastic visitors.

MUSEUM OF FLIGHT

9404 East Marginal Way South • Seattle, Washington • 98108 • (206) 764-5700

GUIDE TO THE RED BARN

Viewed from above, the Museum of Flight shows a physical orientation unlike that of any other aviation museum. Bordered on the east by King County International Airport, and to the south by the massive flight research facilities of the Boeing Company, the Museum's bright Red Barn and ultra-modern Great Gallery are important landmarks in the center of an already-existing environment of takeoffs and landings.

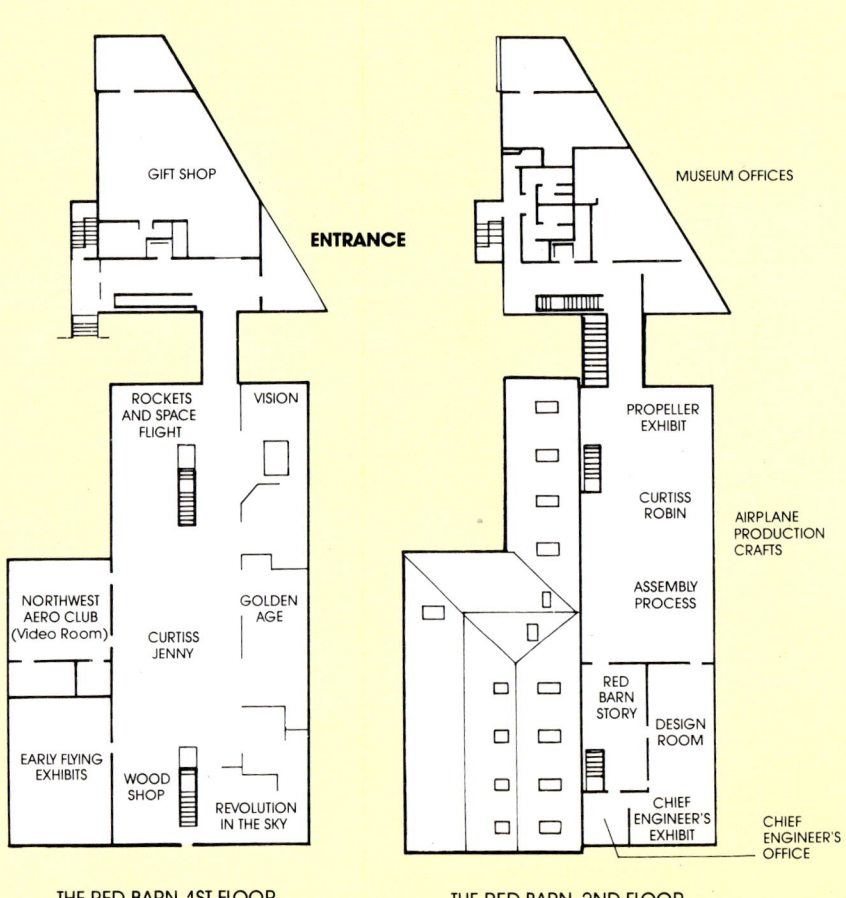

THE RED BARN, 1ST FLOOR

THE RED BARN, 2ND FLOOR

MUSEUM IN PROGRESS

Which was the bigger challenge: restoring a historic wood-frame building like the Red Barn or building a totally new structure of glass and steel to house more than thirty full-size aircraft and a range of interpretive exhibits? Both tasks were more than capably handled by Seattle architect Ibsen Nelsen, whose team of designers and builders turned the dreams of the Museum of Flight Foundation into reality in less than thirteen years. Those dreams, however, are still far from fulfilled. With the help of Aldrich/Pears, a Vancouver, British Columbia, exhibits design firm, the Museum's ambitious vision continues to take form. As each new display and interactive element is brought on line, Museum goers can expect to gain fresh insights into the phenomenon called flight.

GUIDE TO THE GREAT GALLERY

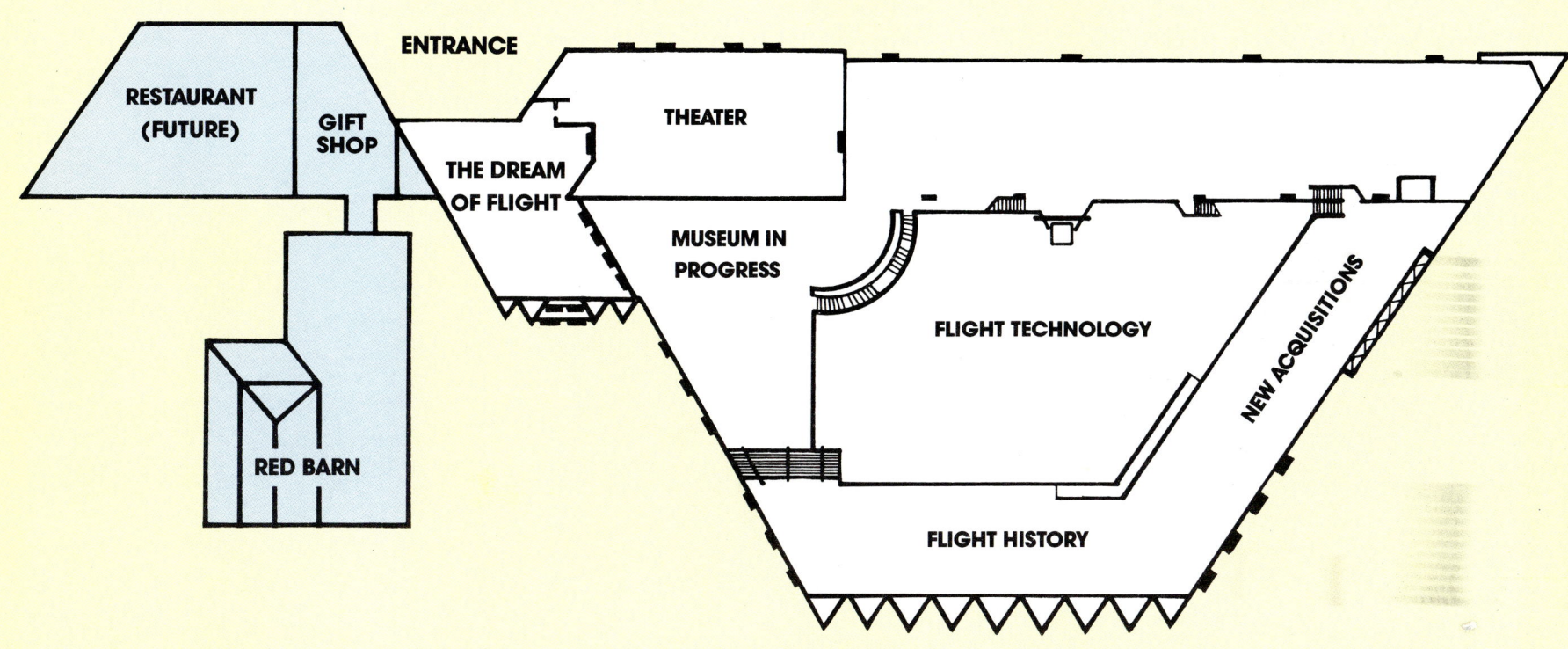

THE · AIRFIELD · AND · BEYOND

INDOOR EVENTS

Guests of the Museum of Flight are invited to take part in the many special events and outreach programs offered. Movies with flight themes are regularly screened in the 268-seat William M. Allen Theater. Hits in the past have included such Hollywood classics as *Captains of the Clouds* and *Twelve O'Clock High*. Visitors are also invited to take guided tours conducted by trained docents, regional experts in the rich history of the aerospace industry, and to attend lectures by noted authorities in the world of aviation.

The Northwest Aero Club meeting room is a popular spot for aviation events (above). In the William M. Allen Theater audiences can choose from contemporary feature films like Top Gun *to inspirational classics such as* Lilac Time, *produced in 1928 (left). The gift shop is full of hard-to-find items—flight jewelry, posters, books, T-shirts and an assortment of handsome emblems and patches (right).*

THE GIFT SHOP

The Museum's gift shop contains one of the best selections of flight-related gifts anywhere. T-shirts, posters, patches, pins and model airplanes are among the many aviation-related items that can be purchased there.

MUSEUM · OF · FLIGHT

THE ARCHIVES

The Museum's aviation archive is the largest on the West Coast. Its shelves overflow with more than thirteen thousand books, videotapes and films. Available to researchers by appointment, the archive also contains more than sixty thousand flight magazines and professional journals, a huge collection of historical photographs and an extensive assortment of items that archivists call "ephemera"— priceless artifacts such as vintage bubblegum cards or the silver-toed cowboy boots of test pilot "Tex" Johnston. If the answer to a question about aviation cannot be found here, it is either classified information or it simply does not exist.

A staff member displays the boots of test pilot "Tex" Johnston (right). Archival materials range from vintage periodicals and publications (left) to bubblegum cards (below), and other flight-related treasures.

THE · AIRFIELD · AND · BEYOND

A young artist gives an interpretation of the Great Gallery (left). Many people find that weekend programs are the perfect way to get the whole family involved (right and below).

MUSEUM · OF · FLIGHT

KIDS LOVE THE MUSEUM OF FLIGHT

The Museum of Flight is a favorite with children, and many entertaining programs are planned just for them. Every Saturday, "Make It and Take It" workshops teach kids how to build and fly their own aviation creations. Two or three times a month, family-theme weekends are held, giving the whole family a chance to learn how to build and fly kites, ultralights, models and other experimental aircraft. Summer is an especially fun time for kids, with special events, field trips, workshops and lectures offered by the Museum.

The Museum's workshops appeal to fliers of all ages; children build their own model airplanes and send them soaring.

THE · AIRFIELD · AND · BEYOND

A visit to the Museum of Flight (above) can often result in surprises. Museum-sponsored rocketry workshops (left) are explosive entertainment.

MUSEUM · OF · FLIGHT

MORE THAN A FABULOUS COLLECTION OF AIRPLANES

With the comings and goings at King County International Airport, and acquisitions like the flyable B-17 at its command, the Museum of Flight is in a prime position to share the excitement of winged flight with the world. One visit should convince you that there is more to the Museum than its extensive collection of aircraft.

One favorite annual event is the "Emerald City Flight Festival," which is a family-oriented aviation celebration that features an airshow, concerts, food and hands-on activities.

Public appearances by such colorful legends as "Wrong Way Corrigan," the test crew of the Boeing 747 and Brigadier General Robert Lee Scott, Jr., author of *God Is My Copilot*, have drawn enthusiastic audiences. Another extremely popular event was the Second Great International Paper Airplane Contest, which attracted flight fans from as far away as Japan.

Following his appearance at the Museum of Flight, Brigadier General Robert Lee Scott, Jr. (left), posed with his favorite World War II fighter, the P-40 Warhawk (above).

THE · AIRFIELD · AND · BEYOND

FLYING FORTRESS

"With wings punctured and ablaze, tail surfaces shredded, with chunks of its graceful body gouged by cannon fire, flak or midair collision, the B-17 brought them home."

— Edward Jablonski
The Flying Fortress

It has been more than fifty years since the Boeing 299, prototype of the legendary precision bomber of World War II, thundered across the Seattle sky. Yet fans of the B-17 Flying Fortress still brag of its achievements in the present tense.

The Museum of Flight is fortunate to have a fully flyable B-17F in its collection. This handsome four-engine monoplane is one of only a dozen such flyable craft in the world. Purchased for the Museum by museum trustee and aviator Bob Richardson in May 1985, the bomber rolled off the Boeing assembly line on February 13, 1943. Within a month it was delivered to Wright Field in Dayton, Ohio, then later reassigned to the Army Air Forces base at Moses Lake, Washington. Its postwar career included a stint as a crop duster in Yakima, Washington, a firefighting borate bomber in Phoenix, Arizona, and a supporting actor in the films *Tora, Tora, Tora* and *The Thousand Plane Raid*.

Few aircraft carry the reputation of the Museum's B-17F Flying Fortress (above), a powerful war machine that could withstand the fiercest aerial opposition of World War II (right). A special patch commemorates fifty years of B-17 bravado (above right).

The Museum of Flight obtains its aircraft in a number of ways—through private donations, direct purchases and corporate gifts. How the Museum acquired its FG-1D Corsair is quite a tale. The inverted gull-wing World War II fighter from Fighter Squadron 774 of the U.S. Navy was pulled from the bottom muck of Seattle's Lake Washington in 1983. Thirty-three years earlier, the plane was en route to the Navy Air Station at Sand Point when it crashed and sank in 150 feet of water. A team of scuba divers from two local firms used air bags, a crane and a miniature submarine to lift the aircraft to the surface. The Corsair is now being restored in Idaho.

How many airplanes have survived thirty-three years of total submersion in a freshwater lake? The Museum's FG-1D Corsair was plucked from Lake Washington in 1983 (left). When restored to its former glory (above), the Corsair will be a priceless component of Museum of Flight exhibitry.

THE · AIRFIELD · AND · BEYOND

the 247D is well worth the tens of thousands of dollars—and an equal number of man-hours—needed to bring the venerable flyer back to life.

It is occasionally almost as hard to restore an airplane as it is to build a new one. To volunteer workers at the Everett hangar, the whole thing is a labor of love. Early in the project, when they took apart the 247D's wing, they found spars almost eaten through with rust. The aluminum alloys in its skin had become brittle, its rivets were cracked and the entire airplane suffered from extensive corrosion, no doubt related to the acidic chemicals used in crop dusting and cloud seeding. Now in its seventh year of renovation, the restoration project of the Museum's 247D is nearing completion and the airplane is scheduled to fly by 1989.

Extensive restoration work on the 247D, lovingly conducted by volunteers at Everett, Washington's, Paine Field (left) is needed before the Museum of Flight can add this spectacular airplane to its collection.

HOW THE MUSEUM OF FLIGHT SELECTS ITS AIRPLANES

The wealth of winged material in the Museum's backyard is deceptive; not every aircraft is worthy of inclusion in an aviation display. Working from a "collections plan" compiled by the Museum of Flight curators, the staff weighs factors such as historical importance, educational value, availability and overall physical condition before adding airplanes to their collection.

Some aircraft, like the Stinson SR Reliant, have come directly into the collection from service. A mimimum of restoration work was required before the Museum could suspend this classic bush plane from the ceiling of the Great Gallery "as is." Others, like the Boeing 247D currently housed in a hangar at Everett, Washington's, Paine Field, require extensive reconstruction. Built in 1933, this all-metal aircraft was very advanced for its time. It was capable of cruising at 175 miles per hour—nearly twice the speed of other commercial craft of its day— and could perform a variety of roles, from carrying passengers to dusting crops or seeding clouds to make rain.

In addition to its obvious historical merit, the Museum's 247D is a rarity. Only three other 247s still exist, the property of the Smithsonian's National Air and Space Museum and similar facilities in Canada and England. Curators feel

A truly innovative aircraft, the Boeing 247D (above) led the way with substantial improvements in transportation design and construction.

CHAPTER THREE

THE AIRFIELD AND BEYOND

The Museum of Flight's Added Attractions

"Building a dream? Easy. A little vision, lots of work, a dash of design excellence, a buck here and a million there, and there you are. Nothing to it."

—Howard Lovering
Museum of Flight
Executive Director

Daily arrivals of an impressive array of aircraft make the Museum of Flight an airplane watcher's paradise—both inside and out (top and bottom).

Situated on the southwest edge of King County International Airport (also known as Boeing Field), the Museum of Flight offers aviation buffs a rare opportunity to get close to the action. In fact, it is often a challenge for visitors to tell where the airfield begins and the Museum's exhibits end. Many special events are held at Boeing Field, featuring everything airborne—from paper airplanes to the Concorde.

Hundreds of airplane enthusiasts gathered one afternoon in November 1984 to cheer the supersonic jet airliner Concorde as it touched down at King County International Airport, making its first West Coast appearance almost on the doorstep of the Museum of Flight.

"The crowd jammed into the valley to await the arrival of the Great Bird," reported the *Highline Times,* a Burien, Washington, newspaper. "People stood atop roofs, along roadways, even spilling out onto the strip where the bird would land, shading their eyes as they intently watched the skies."

The Concorde's arrival was just one of more than 350,000 takeoffs and landings in the Museum's "backyard" that year. Among the fifteen busiest airports in the nation, King County International is a center for small-craft activities in the Northwest, a central point for air express operations and the primary flight test center for the Boeing Company. It is a place where representative aircraft from nearly every continent, class and stage of development arrive and depart each day.

So bring your binoculars—on a good day you might see an airliner from Thailand, a trio of futuristic corporate Lear Jets or a vintage P-51D Mustang taxiing past the windows of the Museum's eastern face.

MUSEUM · OF · FLIGHT

Among the many prestigious arrivals at King County Airport has been the supersonic jet airliner Concorde of British Airways (above), which touched down in November 1984 (right).

WINGS · OVER · THE · WORLD

SEEKERS

"What is it, I wondered, that makes a man willing to sit up on top of an enormous Roman candle, such as a Redstone, Atlas, Titan or Saturn rocket, and wait for someone to light the fuse?"
— Tom Wolfe
The Right Stuff

While the rules of flight—weight, lift, thrust and drag—are still in effect, aviation has changed considerably.

Progress takes place not only in hangars, on airstrips or among the clouds. It is also found in the high-tech laboratories of physicists, cyberneticians and computer scientists. It even touches the silent void of outer space.

The world of flight is still open to anyone who wishes to fly, and is no less accessible than in the early days of the Boeing Airplane Company, when planes were built in a barn and flown by fledgling Navy recruits.

The future of aviation belongs to the seekers—people who have broadened our knowledge by breaking successive barriers of flight.

Seekers have taken the old, global perspectives on flight and given them new, interplanetary meanings. Back on earth, supersonic aircraft like the SR-71 (right) continue to prove that the race belongs to the swift.

35

FLYING FOR FUN

"My underlying philosophy can be summarized as adapting the machine to its builder-pilot and his passengers instead of making them conform to the machine."

— Bill Durand
**Sport Aviation
November, 1978**

The owners of sailplanes, hang gliders and ultralights savor the sensations of soaring with eagles and hawks. Gliders came of age in the 1920s in Germany and in the 1930s in the United States. Sailplanes, with more modern, longer-winged bodies built of fiberglass, became popular in the 1950s and '60s. These flyers were supplemented by hang gliders, controllable one-person "kites" like the Eipper Cumulus, which could be easily carried to a launch site on top of a car, then assembled in minutes using simple tools. Next to appear were the ultralights, which are basically motorized hang gliders that can fly significant distances. The Museum of Flight's Cascade Kasperwing 180-B utilizes the basic flying wing configuration developed by designer/inventor Witold Kasper. Driven by a twenty-three horsepower Zenoah engine, it boasts a comfortable cruising speed of thirty-three miles per hour and a climb rate of eight hundred feet per minute.

An amateur aircraft design is limited only by the budget and the imagination of its builder. A tail-first airplane that appears to back through the sky, another with a fuselage that resembles a dolphin leaping, and the *Voyager*, the only airplane ever to fly nonstop around the world without aerial refueling, are a trio of designs springing from the mind of Burt Rutan. Sleek, attractive Rutan homebuilts in the Museum's collection include the Vari-Eze, a fiberglass and foam two-seater with an uncanny range of seven hundred miles, and the first kitbuilt Quickie ever to fly. Rutan airplanes have set numerous records, and have attracted a following of more than thirty-five hundred hobbyists, who have ordered plans to build their own Rutan aircraft.

The Vari-Eze (left) is one of several creatively designed and constructed homebuilts on display at the Museum of Flight. Equally imaginative designs for ultralights (top) and gliders (above) have greatly expanded the horizons of personalized flight.

WINGS · OVER · THE · WORLD

The Museum also has two propeller-driven World War II fighters in its collection. Its Grumman F4F Wildcat is on loan to an East Coast museum, while its Vought FG-1D Corsair is currently under restoration.

While the Museum's collection contains a number of famous fighters (above left), a favorite with visitors is the Grumman F9F-8 Cougar (opposite page). The Skyhawk (above) was recenty retired from the Blue Angels, the legendary precision flight demonstration team of the U.S. Navy (left).

FIGHTERS

*"Oh! I have slipped the surly bonds of earth
And danced the skies on laughter-silvered wings;*

*Sunward I've climbed, and joined the tumbling mirth
Of sun-split clouds — and done a hundred things
You have not dreamt of..."*

— John Gillespie Magee, Jr.

Out of the ashes of World War II sprung a generation of fighters that changed military history. During the advance into Hitler's Reich, both U.S. and Soviet battalions captured files detailing the design of the Messerschmit Me 262, the world's first operational jet aircraft. The race to produce a superior jet fighter was on.

The Grumman F9F Panther was developed for the lightning-fast aerial confrontations with Russian-built MiG-15s and Yak-9s of the Korean War. Later, the Grumman F9F-8 Cougar with its lengthened fuselage, thinner, swept wings, and a one thousand pound increase in thrust, could travel about 125 miles per hour faster than its Panther predecessor.

Designed originally for aircraft-carrier launched operations, the Douglas A-4F Skyhawk quickly earned its reputation as the U.S. Navy's hot-rod attack airplane. Indeed, the Skyhawk was a natural performer. Powered by a red-hot Pratt & Whitney turbo-jet engine, it could achieve a maximum sea-level speed of 675 miles per hour and a range of seven hundred statute miles. The Skyhawk's ease of handling made an immediate impression on the Blue Angels, the Navy's precision flight demonstration team—as well as with awestruck audiences who watched the Museum's bright blue A-4F for twelve years, before its retirement in 1986.

WINGS · OVER · THE · WORLD

Powered by three Pratt & Whitney 525-hp Hornet engines, the Museum's reconstructed Boeing 80-A (above left) could carry eighteen passengers and 898 pounds of cargo. Pampered passengers (left) could enjoy a wealth of luxuries—from leather-upholstered seats to hot and cold running water. The thrill of flying was now something everyone could enjoy (above right).

TRANSPORTS

"It was with a touch of regret that we clambered out of the plane. The flight was over. We were mere mortals walking upon the earth again."
— *Early airline passenger*

In the early years of flight, adventuresome passengers bought tickets to ride on regularly scheduled mail runs, and savored this once-in-a-lifetime experience atop a pile of mail bags in a frigid cargo hold. However, with the advent of the Model 80, the twelve-passenger trimotor transport of the Boeing Company, passenger travel changed forever. Suddenly there were comfortable leather upholstered seats, individual reading lamps, hot and cold running water, and forced-air ventilation.

On board the Boeing trimotor was one final refreshing "first"—a team of registered nurses known as stewardesses, who poured coffee from a silver service and attended to passengers' needs.

The Model 80-A, produced one year later, was an even greater improvement, carrying eighteen passengers and 898 pounds of cargo coast to coast in a mere twenty-seven hours. Yet it, too, was destined to be outdistanced by aircraft like the Douglas DC-2, the first in a hallowed line of derivatives. The Museum's vintage 80A-1 performed faithfully, first as a carrier of passengers and later as a cargo plane in Alaska, before it was put out to pasture. Rescued from a garbage heap in Anchorage in 1965 and meticulously reconstructed over several years, it is now one of the Museum's most treasured artifacts.

Boeing 80-As landed at Seattle's Boeing Field (left) and at airports across the country. Needs of passengers were attended to by flight attendants who were registered nurses (above).

WINGS · OVER · THE · WORLD

CURATOR'S FAVORITES

BOWERS FLY BABY 1-A

DESIGNER: Peter M. Bowers
BUILDER: Al Stabler, Seattle, WA; 1962
WINGSPAN: 28'
LENGTH: 18' 10 ½"
GROSS WEIGHT: 925 lbs.
POWERPLANT: 65-85-hp Continental engine
TOP SPEED: 115 mph

Ever since the Fly Baby won the Experimental Aircraft Association competition, this handsome, easy-to-assemble airplane has captured the hearts of home builders, who have bought more than four thousand copies of the Fly Baby's plans.

BOEING P-12 (MODEL 100)

MANUFACTURER: Boeing Airplane Company, Seattle, WA; 1929
WINGSPAN: 30'
LENGTH: 20'1"
GROSS WEIGHT: 2,536 lbs.
POWERPLANT: 450-hp P & W R-985 Wasp Jr.
TOP SPEED: 165 mph

Superior design and innovations like the steel and aluminum tubing of its fuselage structure made the P-12 one of the most widely used fighters of its time. Later versions had all-metal, semi-monocoque fuselages.

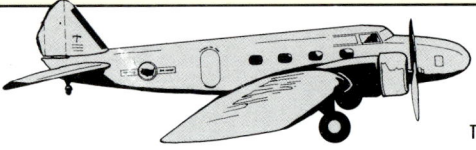

BOEING 247D

MANUFACTURER: Boeing Airplane Company, Seattle, WA; 1933
WINGSPAN: 74'
LENGTH: 51' 7"
GROSS WEIGHT: 12,372 lbs.
POWERPLANT: Two 550-hp P & W Wasp S1H1-G nine cylinder radial engines.
TOP SPEED: 200 mph

The first modern airliner, the 247 was well ahead of its time—in fact, an order for sixty of these all-metal planes was placed before it had passed its mock-up stage.

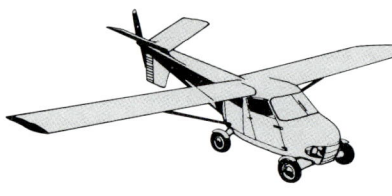

AEROCAR III

MANUFACTURER: Aerocar, Inc., Longview, WA; 1968
WINGSPAN: 34'
LENGTH: 23'
GROSS WEIGHT: 2,100 lbs.
POWERPLANT: 140-hp Lycoming engine
TOP SPEED: 137 mph

Moulton B. Taylor's sporty red Aerocar was certified by the CAA (now the FAA) as an airworthy design—and it could change back into a car in only ten minutes.

HELICOPTERS

"A horse wagon needs a road. The automobile needs a still better road. The railroad needs a track. Airplanes need big airports. But a direct-lift airplane could come in... absolutely anyplace."

— Igor Sikorsky

Victorians imagined that among the travel options in the next century would be the personal helicopter. They envisioned a time when one could simply strap one on and fly. While such notions are still considered flights of fancy, small "sky scooters" like the Museum of Flight's homebuilt RotorWay Scorpion have nearly fulfilled the Victorian prophecy.

The concept of direct lift has captured the imagination of some of the earliest flight innovators. The Russian inventor Igor Sikorsky first experimented with the power of the rotary blade in 1909. Nearly thirty years later, he would overcome obstacles to vertical flight, keeping his prototype VS-300 aloft for an hour and twenty minutes—at the token height of around thirty feet.

In the mid-1940s, Frank Piasecki flew the first tandem-rotor helicopter. Dubbed the Dogship or Flying Banana, it was capable of lifting eighteen hundred pounds—upping the load of Sikorsky's primitive VS-300 by a factor of twenty. A second powerful Piasecki-built craft, the Vertol H-21B Workhorse, lived up to its name. Adopted by the Army at Fort Lewis, Washington, the Workhorse could carry a two-man crew plus fourteen soldiers into battle.

Igor Sikorsky provides "ground support" for his assistant Les Morris, the pilot of an early VS-300 helicopter (top). Sikorsky's achievements were soon overshadowed by the accomplishments of the Piasecki H-21B Workhorse (bottom).

| WINGS · OVER · THE · WORLD |

called their Boeing-Stearman N2Ss (Navy equivalent to the PT-13A) the "Yellow Peril"—a fitting nickname for the trainer, with its chrome yellow paint job and potentially dangerous novice pilots at the throttle. One thousand of these primary trainers came off the production line within five months in 1941.

Stearman aircraft, like the PT-13A in the Museum (left), were used extensively for pilot training (above) during World War II.

OFF TO WAR

"The resourcefulness and energy of our people would have had little avail against our enemies if the Army Air Forces had not begun to make preparations for the war long before Pearl Harbor."
—General Hap Arnold

During World War II, the aviation industry once again underwent a period of accelerated growth. Small aircraft manufacturers like Piper, Taylorcraft and Aeronca turned their attention to the production of light aircraft nicknamed "Grasshoppers"—nimble spotters that could fly low over dense jungle brush, ever watchful for hidden gun emplacements, and land on the most hastily constructed airstrips. In addition, Grasshoppers could be built quickly, almost exclusively from non-strategic materials.

Second only to the immediate need for aircraft was the demand for skilled pilots to fly them. Before the war, the U.S. Army Flying School at Randolph Field, near San Antonio, Texas, was turning out five hundred pilots a year—at best a token number compared with the two hundred thousand fearless aviators who fueled the war machine in years to come. Trainer airplanes like the Museum's yellow-winged Boeing-Stearman PT-13A were instrumental in turning raw recruits into "aces" practically overnight. Navy cadets

Fledgling fliers of the U.S. military services took to the skies in unprecedented numbers during World War II. The Fairchild PT-19 Cornell ("PT" for primary trainer) introduced thousands of cadets to the world of flight (above).

THOMAS F. HAMILTON

Thomas F. Hamilton produced his first wooden propeller in 1909. The following year, he opened Hamilton Aero Manufacturing Company, moving from Seattle, Washington, to Vancouver, British Columbia, in 1915. Here, he fine-tuned his propeller-making operation, at the same time teaching cadets of the Royal Canadian Flying Corps to fly. "Hamiltonians" were the propellers of choice during World War I; in the years that followed, the name "Hamilton Standard" came to mean the very best.

EDMUND T. ALLEN

A freelance test pilot in the 1930s, Edmund T. Allen piloted the first flights of no fewer than thirty-four new aircraft, including the Northrop Alpha, Beta and Gamma; the Douglas DC-2; the Lockheed Constellation; and Boeing's XB-15, 314, and 307. His four years as director of Flight and Aerodynamics for the Boeing Company were abruptly terminated in 1943, when an electrical failure caused the engines of a prototype B-29 to catch fire. Allen died in the crash. He was posthumously awarded the Daniel Guggenheim medal in recognition of his role in standardizing methods for test flights.

ROBERT C. REEVE

Robert C. Reeve arrived in Valdez, Alaska, in 1932, after several years of flying in the South American Andes. He rebuilt a wrecked Eaglerock biplane, leased it from its owner, and

launched Reeve Airways. "Anywhere you'll ride, I'll fly," he told the director of the Boston Museum of Science, who wanted a pilot to land him and a full load of equipment at the eighty-five-hundred-foot level of the Walsh Glacier. Reeve continued to run his airline until his death in 1980. His many achievements—among them transforming a single-airplane operation into a successful scheduled airline—have secured Reeve a place in three separate aviation halls of fame.

PATHFINDERS

The history of aviation is made up of individual achievement—the accomplishments of educators, operations chiefs, fabricators, pilots and engineers. Each year, the Museum of Flight identifies as many as five people who have made significant contributions to aerospace development in the Northwest. To date, more than thirty recipients of the Museum's prestigious Pathfinder Award have been named.

■ ELREY "JEP" JEPPESEN

Elrey "Jep" Jeppesen logged twenty thousand flight hours and more than three million miles during his years as a mail pilot with Boeing Air Transport. Whenever he flew, he jotted down details—airport particulars and notes on terrain—in a ten-cent notebook, a practice that helped him stay on course despite the poor navigational systems of his day. It didn't take long for word of Jeppesen's "Little Black Book" to get around. Borrowing $400 to set up shop in the basement of his Cheyenne, Wyoming, home, Jeppesen published his priceless firsthand information in 1934. Today, Jeppesen Airway Manuals are used by all U.S. airlines and many foreign carriers, as well as by an estimated two-thirds of all instrument-qualified private pilots.

■ CLYDE PANGBORN

According to newsman Lowell Thomas, Clyde Pangborn was "a pioneer throwing off the shackles of the ground." It was Pangborn, along with flier Hugh Herndon, who turned an unsuccessful attempt at circumnavigating the globe in record time, into a triumph, completing the first non-stop crossing of the Pacific. And it was Pangborn who drew America's attention to aviation, carrying more than a half-million passengers during his years as a barnstormer, dedicating some three hundred airports, and traveling around the country—and around the globe—in the 1930s.

WINGS · OVER · THE · WORLD

FRONTIERS OF FLIGHT

"I learned to fly in Dakota, where there's fields everywhere. Here there's nothing but swamps, brush, spruce timber and mountains."

— Art Samson, bush pilot

With the exception of the dogsled, no single mode of transportation opened up the Alaskan wilderness more than the airplane. Perched on skis, pontoons or wheels, versatile aircraft like the Stinson SR Reliant stood ready to tackle the rigors of the "great land."

A successful bush pilot dealt with gale-force winds, temperatures that ranged from subzero to ninety degrees, and terrain that was as vast as it was unfamiliar. In addition to carrying mail, passengers, furs—and even teams of sled dogs to and from remote destinations—these romantically rugged individualists used their airplanes to provide emergency relief. They served as airborne ambulance drivers and dropped supplies to firefighters.

Even the sturdily built Reliant, with its welded steel tube fuselage and dependable 245-horsepower engine, took more than its share of abuse. Reportedly used by bush pilot Jim Dodson in the 1930s, the Museum's chipped and battered floatplane proudly wears the scars of a long and hard life in Alaska.

Many bush pilots, like the flier of this Bellanca CH (left), had devout followings. Pilots' reputations were based largely on the strengths and weaknesses of their airplanes. Some bush planes, like the Stinson SR (above), were equipped with floats for water landings.

Nimble bush planes could easily touch down at remote settlements previously accessible only to dogsleds or Eskimo kayaks (above).

WINGS · OVER · THE · WORLD

The Taylorcraft A (left) came close to being "every person's airplane," but the forgotten Lincoln Sport of 1924 (above) was less popular.

Old Men, Young Men
EVEN CHILDREN FLY
And All Find **T-CRAFT** Their Best Buy!

GOING IN STYLE

"What with the hiss of air, the clatter of the motor, and that big ship's wheel clutched nervously in your sensitive fingers, you feel a little like Captain Ahab in a storm."

— James Gilbert
Flying Magazine

The aviation industry was eager to trade its "nuts and bolts" image for one of sophistication and style. With a glut of small aircraft on the market, manufacturers had to seek out new customers. The Fairchild Aircraft Company appealed to a new breed of fliers with its alluring Fairchild F-24, a jaunty three-seater produced in 1932. More than six hundred of these popular sport, touring and utility airplanes were produced prior to World War II, and many found acceptance with Hollywood's rising stars. The Museum's warm red and orange F-24 is a modest example of a "flying limo"—it was custom-built for ventriloquist Edgar Bergen.

A second aircraft design found a receptive, monied audience even in the darkest days of the Depression. A total of fifteen hundred Taylorcraft A's were built before 1941. Touted as "a step into the future," the Taylorcraft offered such features as side-by-side seating and dual control wheels. "Even Kids Can Fly," boasted Taylorcraft advertisements, presenting the world's youngest solo pilot, ten-year-old Betty Lee Bennett, as proof of its claim.

The dapper Beechcraft 17 Staggerwing (left) and the 1928 Buhl-Verville Airster (above) appealed to a whole new breed of high-flying "bon vivants."

WINGS·OVER·THE·WORLD

The first mail carriers were short-range biplanes with limited space for cargo. The Stearman C-3 (opposite page, left) and the Curtiss Carrier Pigeon I (opposite page, right) were two of these "early birds."

The Ford Tri-motor (above) and the Boeing 80-A (top right) could carry more mail and fly greater distances than earlier mailplanes which were smaller and lighter. Two of these lightweight predecessors can be found in the Great Gallery (bottom right).

FLYING THE MAIL

"In many ways, these first planes of the airmail service were like a family of small children. We would no sooner get them over the measles than they came down with the mumps."

— Captain Ben Lipsner

While nimble airplanes were winning the war on the Western Front, a second squadron was proving its worth closer to home. America's first airmail service was organized in 1918 under the authority of the U.S. Post Office. By the mid-1920s, fifteen Contract Air Mail routes served the nation, with biplanes like the Museum's silver and blue Swallow—one of the more successful designs of the period—leading the pack of Jennys, Standards, de Havillands and other postwar mail carriers.

Airmail did more than take root; it blossomed. In less than a decade, airmail pilots were transporting seven million pounds of mail each year. The dream of private mail carriers—an airplane capable of handling a sizable cargo—was realized with the production of the Stearman C-3B, whose fighter-like shape and throaty Wright "Whirlwind" engine enabled it to carry a payload of 445 pounds and reach speeds in excess of one hundred miles per hour.

The Museum's restored C-3B was acquired in 1986, after it was flown into Boeing Field from Prosser, Washington. Built in February 1928 it sports a portrait of an Indian chief (the logo of Western Air Express) on its fuselage.

WINGS · OVER · THE · WORLD

build upon the success of the Wright brothers, creating an array of airplanes like the Curtiss JN-4D Jenny, whose fully restored airframe sits uncovered in the Red Barn. The Jenny's lacquered spruce struts and spars, taut flying wires, and longerons of ash and oak reflect the fine craftsmanship that went into America's first airplanes.

As the airplane evolved, so too did its uses. The Curtiss JN-4D Jenny (above) was not only a favorite of pilots during World War I; its postwar fan club also included mail carriers and devil-may-care barnstormers (left).

FLIGHT TAKES OFF

"Now we hold all the records! The largest machine ever handled...the longest time in the air, the smallest angle of descent, and the highest wind!!!"

—*Orville Wright
October 1902*

In 1900, Wilbur and Orville Wright, the young owners of a bicycle shop in Dayton, Ohio, conducted a series of experiments that led to the invention of the airplane. Between 1901 and 1902, they spent thousands of hours testing their simple yet aerodynamically sound airfoils in a makeshift wind tunnel and on the sand dunes of Kitty Hawk, North Carolina. The Museum of Flight's 1902 Glider is a full-size reproduction of one such design.

The two inventors refined their aircraft over time, adding control surfaces and an engine. The first self-sustained flights took place on December 17, 1903. Although the longest flight logged that day lasted a mere fifty-nine seconds and covered a distance of 852 feet, it ushered in an era that changed forever the complexion of manned flight.

Aviators like Louis Blériot, who crossed the English Channel in a monoplane of his own design, would soon extend the height and breadth of aerial achievement. Others would

The Museum's 1902 Glider (above) is an exact reproduction of the minimalist craft that ushered in a new era of flight at Kitty Hawk, North Carolina (right).

CHAPTER TWO

WINGS OVER THE WORLD

A Tour of the Great Gallery

One of North America's most comprehensive collections of full-scale aircraft is contained in the Great Gallery. An innovative truss-suspension system has been used to give visitors the same view that they might enjoy on a runway or in the air.

If the Red Barn is a monument to aviation's formative years, then the Great Gallery, an architectural triumph in glass and steel, is a tribute to the lofty and limitless horizons of flight. Once visitors to the Museum of Flight walk from the simple, wood-frame factory that was once the Boeing Airplane Company, they enter the airy environment of the Great Gallery.

This massive, yet elegant, exhibition space was the inspiration of Seattle architect Ibsen Nelsen. Assembled within the Gallery's three million cubic feet of usable space and bounded by a total of ninety thousand square feet of glass, are aircraft representing significant eras of aviation history.

The aircraft—many suspended from the sixty-five foot ceiling by a specially designed truss system—are the undisputed hallmarks of the Museum collection. Faithfully restored aircraft like the Museum's Boeing 80-A or its Fairchild F-24, full-scale reproductions like the 1902 Wright glider, and one-of-a-kind creations like the Rutan Quickie or the Aerocar III, have been carefully chosen by Museum curators for their unusual historic and inspirational attributes. Every plane in the Museum of Flight collection is a treasure, worthy of hours of study.

But as important as the individual aircraft are the numerous stories surrounding each aspect of flight. The Great Gallery's displays are given extra life through imaginative signage, creative interactive components and specially selected artifacts—important elements that put the airplanes in their proper cultural context. Collectively they reveal the full scope of humankind's longing to fly.

MUSEUM · OF · FLIGHT

HUMBLE · BEGINNINGS

of flight for thousands of years, only in relatively recent times has this dream become a reality.

From the feathered beeswax wings of Icarus to the sophisticated models of Leonardo da Vinci; from the hot air balloons of the Montgolfier brothers to the Wright Flyer —an array of developments has brought us ever closer to achieving our goal of sailing among the stars.

First Parachute Jump
Andre-Jacques Garnerin survives the first human descent in a parachute.

Montgomery Glider
John J. Montgomery designs the first American glider, launching it from a hot air balloon for flights of greater duration.

Wright Flyer
The Wright brothers meet the challenge of manned flight, keeping their propeller-driven Wright Flyer aloft at Kitty Hawk, North Carolina.

First Military Airplane
The Signal Corps of the U.S. Army buys its first aircraft, a Wright Model A Flyer.

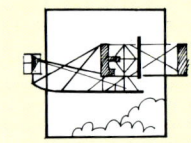

First Transcontinental Airplane Flight
Calbraith Rogers flies across the United States. The trip takes him forty-nine days.

1797 A.D.   1852 A.D.   1884 A.D.   1891-96 A.D.   1903 A.D.   1906 A.D.   1908 A.D.   1909 A.D.   1911 A.D.   1914 A.D.

Giffard's Dirigible
Henri Giffard successfully launches the first navigable airship, a steam-driven dirigible with a primitive propeller.

Lilienthal Gliders
German inventor and engineer Otto Lilienthal experiments with curved-wing glider designs, performing close to two thousand trials before ending his innovative career with a fatal crash.

First Powered Airplane Flight in Europe
Alberto Santos-Dumont, a Brazilian living in Paris, conducts the first test flight of a powered airplane in Europe, staying aloft for eight seconds.

Blériot Flies Airplane Across English Channel
Louis Blériot flies a monoplane from Calais to Dover.

First Scheduled U.S. Airline
The Benoist Company inaugurates the first regularly-scheduled passenger airline service in the world, flying between St. Petersburg and Tampa, Florida.

THE HISTORY OF FLIGHT

"How I yearn to throw myself into endless space and float above the awful abyss."
— Johann Wolfgang von Goethe

The founders of the Boeing Airplane Company pursued the same dream and were bound by the same conventions and constraints as the earliest aviators. While humankind has been obsessed with the notion

Egyptian Winged Gods
Winged gods Isis and Horus are worshipped throughout the Egyptian Empire.

Invention of the Kite
Chinese builders perfect the first bamboo and paper kites.

"Winged Victory" Statue
An unknown sculptor on the island of Samothraki in Greece carves the statue of the goddess Nike. This statue, reconstructed from 118 separate pieces, is now known as "Winged Victory of Samothrace."

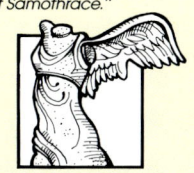

Leonardo da Vinci Models
Inspired Italian Leonardo da Vinci creates numerous models of flying machines.

Montgolfier Brothers' Balloon
The Montgolfiers, a pair of French brothers, construct and launch the first balloon capable of carrying animals and humans.

| 1200 B.C. | 1100 B.C. | 1000 B.C. | 900 B.C. | 180 B.C. | 1100 A.D. | 1500 A.D. | 1670 A.D. | 1783 A.D. | 1785 A.D. |

Icarus and Daedalus
Legendary aviators Icarus and Daedalus build feathered wings to soar from the Island of Crete.

Hermes and Mercury
Winged mythological figures Hermes and Mercury are depicted in Roman and Greek temple art.

Gunpowder Rockets
Chinese warlords use gunpowder rockets attached to arrows and spears to disrupt troops and set fire to buildings.

De Lana "Vacuum Balloon"
Francesco De Lana drafts plans for the "vacuum balloon," considered to be the first rational design for a lighter-than-air craft.

Blanchard and Jeffries Cross English Channel
Jean-Pierre Blanchard and Dr. John J. Jeffries sail from England to France, crossing the English Channel in a balloon.

HUMBLE · BEGINNINGS

■ AERONAUTICAL CONCEPTS

"Learning the secret of flight from a bird was a good deal like learning the secret of magic from a magician. After you know what to look for, you see things that you did not notice when you did not know exactly what to look for."

—Orville Wright

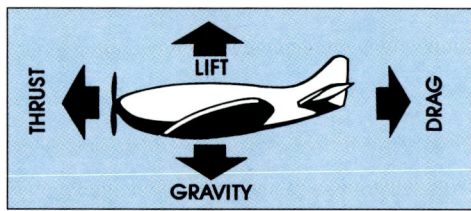

FOUR FACTORS OF FLIGHT

WEIGHT includes the airplane, its fuel and its "payload"—either passengers, cargo or both.

LIFT is the force by which an airplane overcomes the pull of gravity.

DRAG is a measure of resistance created by the air surrounding the aircraft.

THRUST is the force that overcomes drag and moves the airplane forward.

Weight, a component of gravity, is probably the easiest factor for most of us to understand—it is a limitation we have dealt with ever since we could crawl! But for birds or humans to soar, they must overcome their own weight and the down-to-earth influence of gravity.

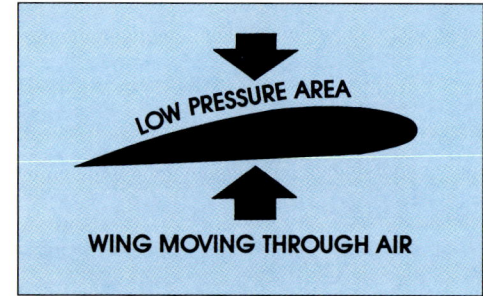

WING SHAPE

Lift, too, is an easy concept to understand—an airplane is literally "lifted" into the air by wind passing over its wings. Air traveling over the curved wing of the plane moves faster than the air underneath, making the pressure on top less than that on the bottom. As the wing is forced upward, it carries the airplane with it. The faster an airplane moves (the greater its thrust), the more lift is created, and the easier it is for a pilot to overcome gravity and drag.

CONTROLS

Of course, full mastery of the sky requires more than an understanding of four fundamental forces. A basic set of controls allows the pilot to choose how, when and where these four forces are applied, and to set or change the airplane's flight path at will. While aircraft designs have changed radically since the days of the Wright brothers, the controls—the throttle, elevators, rudder and ailerons—have remained more or less the same.

11

An initial order from the U.S. Navy for two C series airplanes preceded America's entry into World War I. The Navy soon upped its order to fifty of the trainers, and by the summer of 1917, some three hundred workers were added to meet Boeing's rigorous production schedule.

All but one of the fifty-six C series airplanes used twin pontoons—the sole exception was kept afloat by a single main pontoon and small auxiliary floats under each wingtip. This modification enabled the Navy to prepare its pilots for duty on battleships and cruisers, where airplanes were launched by catapult. Two additional experimental landplanes, custom-built for the U.S. Army, featured auxiliary nose wheels and side-by-side seating.

Upon completion of the 1917 Navy order, an additional C was built by Boeing. This airplane carried the first U.S. International Contract Air Mail from Seattle, Washington, to Victoria, British Columbia, on March 3, 1919.

A C Series trainer airplane in flight.

HUMBLE · BEGINNINGS

first hops in the B & W on June 15, 1916. Test flights were conducted in August 1916 by Knox Martin, who gave the biplane a clean bill of health. "The tests were satisfactory in every respect," he reported to William Boeing. By the end of the year, the B & W had made eighty-two flights, logging nearly thirty hours in the air.

The Museum of Flight's replica B & W was built in 1966 for the Boeing Company's golden anniversary. The use of steel tubing and revised tail surfaces make it structurally different from the original plane. Its temperamental engine has been replaced by a 170-horsepower Lycoming, a modern upgrade that gives the replica a cruising speed of 65 mph.

A succession of Navy trainers, the C series airplanes, followed the B & W. Versatile, well-built biplanes, these were the first "all-Boeing" creations, owing little to the designs put forth by other aviation companies.

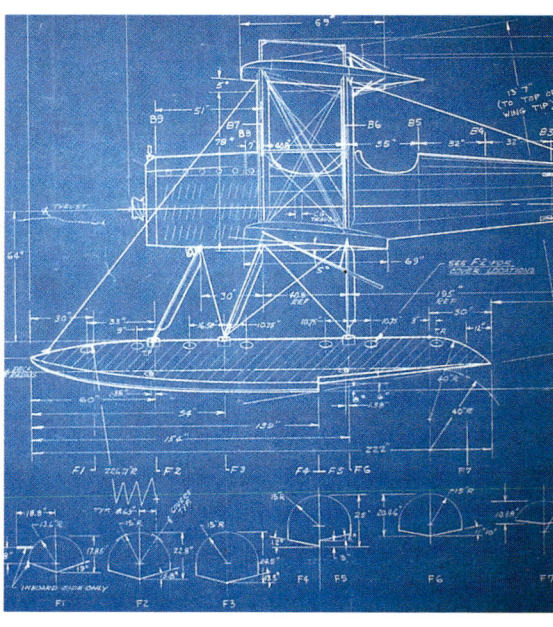

The Museum's replica B & W (left) was meticulously assembled from plans like the detailed blueprints shown above.

Whether at rest at Seaplane Station on the shores of Lake Union (opposite page, left) or soaring toward the clouds (opposite page, right), the B & W quickly won the hearts of Seattle aviators.

MUSEUM · OF · FLIGHT

THE FIRST BOEING AIRPLANES

"I hope for great things from our new model machine and will be greatly disappointed if it does not prove valuable for defensive purposes."

— William Boeing

The first airplane built in the Red Barn was the B & W, named after company founder William E. Boeing and George C. Westervelt, a U.S. Navy engineering officer who assisted in its construction.

The owner of a 1915 Martin TA seaplane, William Boeing was all too familiar with its limitations. He submitted his preliminary designs for a new, improved seaplane to engineers at MIT, who ran stress-analysis and wind-tunnel experiments, producing a considerably lighter plane with a greater wingspan than the Martin. The aircraft's vertical tail was enlarged to improve lateral stability, and a pair of sixteen-foot pontoons replaced the Martin's single float.

Herb Munter, one of the first fliers of the Martin TA, affectionately called the B & W's 125-horsepower engine a "cast-iron queen." Its undependable nature, however, caused other fliers to describe the six-cylinder powerplant in less-glowing terms. William Boeing made the

HUMBLE · BEGINNINGS

THE BOEING EXECUTIVE CLASS, CIRCA 1919

Edward Hubbard (left) and William E. Boeing (right).

■ William E. Boeing
Boeing Airplane Company Founder

Few men have had an impact on an American industry to the extent that William Boeing did on aviation. The only son of German immigrants, Boeing left Yale University and moved to Seattle in 1903. He founded the Boeing Airplane Company in 1916; within fourteen years the company had become one of the largest aircraft plants in the nation.

■ Edward Hubbard
Airmail Pilot

Edward Hubbard joined the Boeing Company as a test pilot at the close of World War I. When Boeing Air Transport was formed, he was appointed first vice president in charge of mail between Oakland, California, and Chicago, Illinois.

■ Philip G. Johnson
President

A bright, young engineering student recruited from the University of Washington in 1917, Johnson rose quickly through the ranks. In 1926, when he was only thirty-one years old, he became president of the company.

■ Clairmont L. Egtvedt
Chief Engineer

Egtvedt joined the Boeing Airplane Company in 1917 as a draftsman. During his prolific career as chief engineer, he was responsible for the design of the Model 40, the Model 80 and the development of the B-17. He later became vice president, president, and, finally, chairman of the board.

■ Louis S. Marsh
Mechanical Engineer

One of Boeing's first three engineers, Marsh's ground-breaking research in metals led to the design of the Boeing Monomail, an all-metal transport airplane that would revolutionize modern aviation design forever.

The orderly desk of Clairmont Egtvedt, Chief Engineer of the Boeing Airplane Company, is an inspiration to up-and-coming flight engineers visiting the Red Barn (above).

During its heyday, the Red Barn's lower floor contained a woodworking area, bench shop, glue room and propeller department. Sounds of hammers, saws, woodplanes and drills permeated the partitioned offices of engineers, draftsmen and technicians on its upper floor.

Across the way in the new assembly plant, a team of ten women sewed fabric covers onto wooden wing frames. It took ten days to complete a single wing. Each wing received a coat of banana oil, the fumes of which were easily carried aloft. Eventually the aromatic oil coated each unprotected surface of the drafty Red Barn.

In less than three years, the Red Barn's ranks swelled to three hundred full-time workers. In 1928, the *Christian Science Monitor* called the Red Barn complex "the largest factory in the U.S. devoted exclusively to the manufacture of aircraft."

But even the *Monitor's* reporters couldn't forecast the growth of the Boeing Airplane Company over the next fifty years. Today the Boeing Company is a multibillion-dollar concern. Spread over fifty million square feet of space, its five separate plants currently employ a total of more than eighty-nine thousand people in the Seattle area.

No longer the hub of Boeing's thriving industry, the Red Barn remains a strikingly accurate monument to the early days of aviation. A treasured landmark on the National Historic Register, it has been skillfully restored to serve as a focal point for the Museum of Flight.

Teams of skilled woodworkers (top) turned out quality airplane parts on the first floor of the Red Barn. These well-wrought propellers (bottom right) are evidence of their ingenuity. Museum visitors (bottom left) savor a moment at the Red Barn.

Then and now: the fully restored Red Barn (top) and a glimpse of the plant as it stood in the early 1920s (bottom).

CHAPTER ONE

HUMBLE BEGINNINGS

The Boeing Airplane Company Takes Off

"We are embarked as pioneers upon a new science and industry in which it behooves no one to dismiss any novel idea with the statement that 'it can't be done'."
— William Boeing

It was the spring of 1916, a time of warfare and wonderment. As "The Great War" raged overseas, Americans witnessed the unveiling of the world's first electric clock. Lillian Gish starred in the silent screen epic *Intolerance,* and the American Army, led by General John Pershing, chased the outlaw Pancho Villa across the border into Mexico.

On the outskirts of Seattle, Washington, in a small shed on the banks of the Duwamish River, half a dozen employees of the Boeing Airplane Company were hard at work putting the finishing touches on the fledgling factory's first product, a float-equipped biplane called the B & W.

In these early years, the factory—its frame shed, single office building and tool house— saw double duty. It was not only the birthplace of the now-famous Boeing Company, but the workspace of Edward Heath, a master builder contracted six years earlier to construct William Boeing's personal yacht, the "Taconite." Later, as "Captain Ed's" enterprise showed signs of financial ruin, William Boeing stepped in, purchasing the Heath shipyard for "$10 and other considerations." We can presume that Boeing also bought Heath's debts.

William Boeing wasted little time in modifying the shipyard to suit his needs. The factory's old, sloping shipway floor was covered with one of wood, and a second story of offices was added. A tar-papered shed (later replaced by a much larger brick and timber structure) gave builders an additional workspace, while business offices soon occupied a second new building. When the huge barn-like aviation plant was given a fresh coat of red paint, it lived up to its contemporary nickname, "The Red Barn."

5

MUSEUM · OF · FLIGHT

The feel of the historic Red Barn in its heyday (left) is faithfully recreated by imaginative exhibits—full-figure representations of woodworkers (top left) and seamstresses (above) hard at work.

CONTENTS

Chapter ONE
HUMBLE BEGINNINGS
The Boeing Airplane Company Takes Off

Page 4

Chapter TWO
WINGS OVER THE WORLD
A Tour of the Great Gallery

Page 14

Chapter THREE
THE AIRFIELD AND BEYOND
The Museum of Flight's Added Attractions

Page 36

Copyright © 1988 Museum of Flight.
All rights reserved. This book, or parts thereof,
must not be reproduced in any form without permission.

A C K N O W L E D G E M E N T S

Edited by Teresa Roupe. Design by Sarah Fine. Editorial consultation by Carey Vendrame. Production by Karen Hubbard. Production coordination by David Murdock. Editorial assistance by Gilda Parodi-Swords. Typesetting by the TypeStudio, Santa Barbara, CA.

Special thanks to Beau Fong, Victor Seely and Jay Spenser from the Museum of Flight for their participation in this publication. The author would like to acknowledge Drew Ann Wake and Russell Kelly of Aldrich/Pears Associates for research assistance.

Produced by Sequoia Communications
2020 Alameda Padre Serra, Santa Barbara, CA 93103   (805) 963-9336

Printed in Hong Kong   ISBN 0-917859-31-6   First Printing, 1988

P H O T O   C R E D I T S

THE BOEING COMPANY ARCHIVE: 4 bottom left, 5 bottom left, 6 top, 7 top left, top middle, bottom middle, top right, bottom right, 8, 10, 24 middle, 25, 27 right, 31 left, right, 36 right, 38. PETER BOWERS COLLECTION: 17 left. PATRICIA PATTERSON DUDLEY COLLECTION: 30 right. CHRIS EDEN: cover, inside front cover. ELEUTHERIAN MILLS HISTORICAL LIBRARY: 20 right. JOHN LOFASO: 41 right, 45 left, 46 bottom left and right, 47 right. CHARLES McALLISTER COLLECTION: 34 bottom right. MUSEUM OF FLIGHT ARCHIVE: 3, 5 top left, 16 bottom, 17 right, 21 bottom, 24 right, 40 left, 47 middle, back cover. MUSEUM OF MODERN ART: 47 left. NASA: 35 middle and right. MIKE PERRY: 11. JOEL ROGERS: 4 top left and right, 6 bottom left and right, 7 bottom right, 9, 14, 15, 16 top, 19 lower right, 23 right, 27 left, 28 right, 31 top, 32, 33 left and right, 34 left and top right, 37, 39, 41 left, 42, 43, 44, 45 top and bottom right, 46 top right, inside back cover, back flap. SMITHSONIAN INSTITUTION ARCHIVE: 18 right, 19 top right, 20 left, 21 right, 35 left, 36 left. UNITED AIRLINES: 19 left. UNITED TECHNOLOGIES: 28 top left. USAF: 41 middle. U.S. NAVY: 33 inset, 40 right. DAVID WATERSUN: Front flap. GORDON S. WILLIAMS COLLECTION: 18 left, 21 top left, 22 left, 23 left, 26, 30 left.

I L L U S T R A T I O N   C R E D I T S

SARAH FINE: 2, 11, 12, 13, 24. KAREN HUBBARD: 29, 48 and inside back cover.
REBEKKA SJOQUIST, AGE EIGHT, OF BOTHELL, WASHINGTON: 45 left.

MUSEUM OF FLIGHT

Seattle ■ Washington

Written by David G. Gordon